ON HIS WINGS

Inspired Writings
By
Sandra J Yearman

SERAPHIM PUBLISHING LLC

WE WILL BRING LIGHT TO ALL THE DARK PLACES

Registered trademark-
Sandra J Yearman
Seraphim Publishing
438 Water St. Cambridge, WI 53523

Copyright © 2008 Sandra J Yearman
Produced in the United States of America
Author : Sandra J Yearman
Editor: Sandra J Yearman
Cover Design by Sandra J Yearman
Layout and design by Sandra J Yearman

All rights reserved. No part of this book may be reproduced, stored in or introduced into a retrieval system, or transmitted, in any form or by any means, electronic or mechanical, including photocopying or recording or otherwise copied for public or private use—other than for "fair use" as brief quotations embodied in articles and reviews--without written permission from the author.

Library of Congress Control Number: 2009906737
ISBN: 978-0-9815791-7-7
First Edition

Jesus
Your Birth Stopped Time
And Aligned The Worlds
You Walked Among Us As A Man
You Stood Before Us As A God
The World Will Never Know
Another As You
Amen
Amen
Amen

CONTENTS

DEDICATION

The Song Poured Forth...................................7
Jesus Comforts Me..9
The Cry Of Israel..12
As I Prayed Before An Altar............................15
To Look Upon..18
Lord Of Israel..20
The Time Of Heaven Is Here..........................22
Worship...25
Star Of Heaven..27
You Stood Before Me..29
We Are The Children Of God........................31
Walking With Jesus..33
Easter...36
Jesus I Just Want To Thank You.....................38
God Will Always Be There..............................40
Time..42
Angels And Pearls...44

CONTENTS

SEEKING LIGHT IN THE DARKNESS

Jesus Hear Me 48
A Friend 50
The Unheard Screams 52
God, Are There No Warriors 54
I Will Not Fear 56
They Pierced You, My Lord 57
God We Need Your Blessings 59
Healed 62
One Voice Pierced The Darkness 64
Help Her Find The Way 67
Lord Send Me An Angel 69

COMING HOME

Seven Little Angels 71
Brought Me Back To You 74
Bring Me Back To Your Arms 76
I Choose To Ride With King David 78
Darkness Will Never Stop The Dance 79
God Walk With Me 81

Dedication

The Song Poured Forth

The Heavens opened
And the Song poured forth
The music filled the worlds

The lights of Heaven illuminated
The darkest of places

The Son of God was born
In the vessel of mankind
In the frailty of humanity
In a world engulfed with darkness

The Song of Heaven
Transformed the worlds

The melody brought us peace
The notes danced with grace
The precious gift Himself, blessed us
further

He blessed us with Salvation
He blessed us with God's Love
He blessed us with Holy teachings

He blessed us with the chords to the
Song
The chords of faith and forgiveness
The chords of life eternal

Heavenly Father fill us with Your Song
Teach us the words
Heal us
And help us to follow the chords
Home

Amen Amen Amen

Jesus Comforts Me

When I am overwhelmed by the trials
of life
My dreams to nightmares turn
When all my friends have forsaken me
And to change my life I yearn

When I am scared and lonely
And through my tears I can not see
I cry out to the Heavens
And Jesus comforts me

When my grief has over taken
And my life has lost control
When the sorrow is so powerful
That no one can control

When I am scared and lonely
And through my tears I can not see
I cry out to the Heavens
And Jesus comforts me

When my body is broken
And stricken with illness and plight
When I am afraid to sleep
For fear I will die in the night

When I am scared and lonely
And through my tears I can not see
I cry out to the Heavens
And Jesus comforts me

Through the toils and hardships
And through life's labor and pain
Through the broken promises
My courage to regain

When I am scared and lonely
And through my tears I can not see
I cry out to the Heavens
And Jesus comforts me

When death has overtaken
And my eyes no longer see
I will cry out to the Heavens
And Jesus will come for me

Amen Amen Amen

The Cry of Israel

The cry of Israel came to the Lord
The Father heard the Son
The pleas of the children
Voices forever rung

The Father in His Mercy
And His forgiving ways
Took pity on His children
And blessed them in these days

You need not have an army
You need not be a king
You need to have faith in God
For miracles to bring

God chose a Holy man
To use as His light
A man of faith and courage
A man not of the night

God showed Moses miracles
And Moses in his humility
Asked God 'Why have you chosen
A simple man as me'

You need not have an army
You need not be a king
You need to have faith in God
For miracles to bring

God ignited a Holy Fire
In Moses on that day
The day he saw the bush
The day he learned to pray

Moses led God's children
Away from hell's dark door
He led them to the Promised Land
And he gave them so much more

You need not have an army
You need not be a king
You need to have faith in God
For miracles to bring

For as they wandered
As they walked
Moses sang God's Song
God's word he taught

God is always with us
The Father hears the Son
Cry out to the Heavens
Be blessed by the Holy One

You need not have an army
You need not be a king
You need to have faith in God
For miracles to bring

Amen Amen Amen

As I Prayed Before An Altar

As I prayed before an altar
I heard the Angels sing
Their voices moved within me
Lost memories, to begin

The candles flickered slowly
Their flames danced to the Holy sound
Music sent from Heaven
Blessings that abound

The music overtook me
I was helpless in its spell
I felt the Spirit move within me
Home to Heaven I would dwell

As I prayed before an altar
I heard the Angels sing
Their voices moved within me
Lost memories, to begin

The altar that I pray at
Has seen me many days
I kneel before my Savior
I sing with heartfelt praise

But on this Easter morning
I heard the Angels sing
My voice was not alone
The Song of Heaven did ring

As I prayed before an altar
I heard the Angels sing
Their voices moved within me
Lost memories, to begin

When I heard the voices
I was scared and yet I smiled
I knew that God was with me
And that we would walk awhile

Amen Amen Amen

To Look Upon

When I am in my garden
I hear creation's song
As if I leave this world
And Angels walk among

I hear the Heavens whisper
With the uniqueness of what I see
Creation is so complex
I know with certainty

That life was not an accident
An explosion in time and space
I look upon a flower
And I am filled with Holy Grace

To feel the Face of Heaven
To draw God's Presence near
I walk among creation
With faith and without fear

Amen Amen Amen

Lord Of Israel

Chants of the ancients
Goblets of gold
Temple erected
Splendor behold

Sages and prophets
The child-man King
Glory and honor
Psalms did sing

God in His Mercy
Warriors of old
Soared without boundaries
Miracles behold

Balance of branches
Tree of the living
Wisdom of God
Love and forgiving

And through the ages
The ancient truths ring
Glory to God
Father and King

Amen Amen Amen

The Time Of Heaven Is Here

Let the Song of Heaven pour forth
For all creation to hear
The Holy Angels Herald
The Time of Heaven is here

Heaven and earth align
Under the power of the Son
A gift most precious
Given by the Holy One

A Holy child was born
In a world of darkness and hate
The world did not know Him
Many did not accept that He was the
Holy Gate

This precious child
The Savior of mankind
Entered our world as a whisper
Many did not understand the Holy signs

As this whisper
Grew to a roar
He conquered death
He taught us how to soar

He taught us of the Heavens
And the Holy Father Divine
He taught of the Trinity
He showed us the Holy Signs

This precious child was named Jesus
But we know Him by many names
Immanuel, The Shepherd, The
Holy One
They are all one and the same

For does mankind have one word
That can contain and describe
The Holiness of Heaven
The description defies all scribes

Amen Amen Amen

Worship

The God of the ancients
The God of today
He walked with our fathers
He stands before us today

He is Eternal
He is the Way
His Love is forever
He speaks to us this day

Mystery of mysteries
Spirit in Three
Son and the Father
The Door and the Key

Man and the Spirit
Lamb and the Cross
Years turn into centuries
Yet nothing is lost

Miracles and prophesies
Tests of creation
The Father never leaves us
He is our Salvation

The God of the ancients
The God of today
He walked with our fathers
He stands before us today

Amen Amen Amen

Star Of Heaven

God let the star of Heaven
Guide us as it did that night of old
To the Presence of our Savior
Who would break the darkest hold

God let the star we follow
Be the Light that represents
The Holiness of Heaven
The Grace and Love You sent

God in these worlds of darkness
Of shame and horror untold
Let the Holy Star of Heaven
Our pathways to unfold

When darkness overtakes us
And fear and terror fill us with grief
Let the Holy Light of Heaven
Bring this world relief

Amen Amen Amen

You Stood Before Me

You stood before me
You saved my soul

You stood before me
You took my torture

You stood before me
You faced my darkness

You stood before me
And You love me

Lord forgive me
Lord forgive us
Lord forgive our world

Jesus help me to be worthy of
Your Sacrifice
Your Forgiveness
Your Love

Lord give me the faith
Lord give me the strength
Lord give me the love
To stand before You
As You stand before me

Amen Amen Amen

We Are The Children Of God

We are the children of God
We are everywhere

We are dead
We are tortured
We are in darkness

We are scared
We are alone

We are starving
We are in pain
We are abandoned

We are forgotten
We are invisible
We are every where

Jesus deliver us from evil
Jesus conquer the darkness
Jesus save us
Jesus forgive us
Jesus bring us Home

Amen Amen Amen

Walking With Jesus

When loneliness engulfs me
And fear chills me to the bone
When I am afraid that others will hear my cries
And God, I feel so alone

I can not be alone if I walk with Jesus
Lonely I will no longer be
Darkness can not defeat me
Lord I choose to walk with Thee

When my fears have overtaken
And I can no longer speak
When my world is shaken
And I am afraid to seek

I can not be alone if I walk with Jesus
Lonely I will no longer be
Darkness can not defeat me
Lord I choose to walk with Thee

When darkness is my prison
And the sunrise I can no longer see
When I think that God has forsaken
I should cry, Lord to Thee

I can not be alone if I walk with Jesus
Lonely I will no longer be
Darkness can not defeat me
Lord I choose to walk with Thee

For every man creates his prison
And the jailors have lost the keys
Lord lift me from this darkness
Jesus carry me

Amen Amen Amen

Easter

The Song of the stars
The breath of the skies
The mysteries of life
The answer to why

The call of creation
Life's journey without end
The wine of the Heavens
The Savior of men

Timeless, eternal
Heaven behold
King of the worlds
Prophesies foretold

Spirit uplifted
Life without sin
Redeemer most Holy
Life can begin

Amen Amen Amen

Jesus I Just Want To Thank You

Jesus, I just want to thank You
I do not think we take the time
To really thank You for what
You did for us

I hear the words
But I can not imagine
The horror You faced

I hear the words
But I can not imagine
The pain You endured

I hear the words
But I can not imagine
How much You love us

You took our death sentences for us
You took the pain
You took the terror
You took the horror

You stood before us and faced the beast

Amen Amen Amen

God Will Always Be There

God will always be there
Just ask to have Him near
Every one is His child
Every voice He does hear

Even when you whisper
He knows what is in your heart
He listens to our thoughts
Of our lives He should be a part

Call upon the Father
When you have gone a stray
When fear seizes your heart
When you are thankful for the day

Call upon the Holy One
And speak with open heart
Know that He will Love you
And you will never be apart

Amen Amen Amen

Time

Lord, I heard someone say that
everyday we should make time for the
sacred
Every day, every day, every day

Lord, as I thought about this
statement
I realized that every second of our lives
should be for the sacred

That we should not be excluding You
That we should not be making time
for You
That we should ask You to be our daily
lives

Lord, fill me with Your Presence
Consume me with Your Spirit
Engulf me with Your Love

Amen Amen Amen

Angels And Pearls

I have had a love affair with Angels
Since the beginning of my days
I knew I felt their presence
I sensed their Holy ways

My house it is a tribute
To the gifts God sends from above
It is filled with creatures great and small
The forgotten and the unloved

And every room would be naked
If it did not have a symbol of the Lord
An image of an Angel
The cross and the sword

Every Christmas
Miracles behold
When I create a tree of Angels
The tarnished and the gold

Angels of every species
Every description, every right
And I adorn them with pearls and gold
This tree gives great brilliance in the night

Every Angel represents
The Holiness from above
The gifts God sends to us
With Mercy and with Love

Some of my favorite Angels
Are the tattered and the worn
The ones that some humans
Might discard and scorn

Because the gifts that God sends at
Christmas
Can be wrapped in any guise
Ask God to help you see
The Love with Holy eyes

Amen Amen Amen

Seeking Light In The Darkness

Jesus Hear Me

Jesus hear me
I am imprisoned by my own fears
The darkness is as chains that bind me
I can not free myself

I can not fly freely, as You created me
I am bound
I am a prisoner
I am in a cell of darkness and despair

I am not worthy
I am not worthy
I am not worthy

I am so lost in the darkness
I can not find the way out of this prison
My fears are as walls that keep building up around me

Oh Lord, please hear me crying
Oh Lord, please hear me crying
Oh Lord, please hear me crying

Free me from this prison
Free me from bondage
Free me from fear and despair

Take me Home

Amen Amen Amen

A Friend

The world had damaged him greatly
A friend that I would find
They said he was beyond repair
They said a waste of time

I refused to believe what they said
For in my heart I saw
The glimmer of a Holy Light
That would make it worth the all

He was a sign from Heaven
That miracles do abound
With love he was transformed
Through love His life was found

And as our lives developed
We played such similar roles
When one of us was sinking
The other brought us home

His memory never leaves me
Though pictures tear and fray
Lord let me keep the memories
For his presence I would pray

Every gift that God does send us
Is a light in this dark place
Lord, thank You for my friend
Lord, thank You for Your Grace

And to the friends that God sends me
In this life of struggle and pain
Each one is a Holy gift
A loving blessing to gain

Amen Amen Amen

The Unheard Screams

The unheard screams of the dead
Shatter the illusions
Of the worlds they exist in
Of the worlds without reason

Worlds filled with darkness
Created by hatred and fear
Screams of the victims
Does anyone hear

Mankind fears
The wrath of hell
Hell is where we live
Hell is where we dwell

God save Your children
The victims and the warriors
The broken and the healers
Those filled with sorrow

God bring us back
To Your Holy fold
Our Father in Heaven
As the scriptures fore told

God cleanse Your children
Of their hatred and fear
Stop the cries of the victims
Bring the Heavens here

Amen Amen Amen

God, Are There No Warriors

God, are there no warriors in this world
Has darkness compromised integrity
Has darkness destroyed honor

Can man not stand for Your Word
Without substituting His
Prejudices
Bigotry
And hatred

Can man not have the faith and courage
To stand before You
As You stand before us

Can man not have the majesty
To stand against darkness

Can man not learn to overcome
the fears
That bind
That cripple
That rule their behavior

Can man not learn to pray

You gave us the words
God, now please give us the courage to say them

Lord let Thy Kingdom come

Lord let Thy Will be done

For Thine Lord is the Power and the Glory

Amen Amen Amen

I Will Not Fear

I will not hide in fear
Because demons surround me
And the darkness is near

I walk with God at my side
The darkness should cower
The demons should hide

For when I called out God's Name
My life became different
Nothing has remained the same

I call the darkness
To meet me face to face
I do not fear death
I walk with God's Grace

Amen Amen Amen

They Pierced You, My Lord

Darkness pierced the human vessel
Not the Spirit of God

Darkness tore the flesh of frailty
Not the Majesty of Heaven

Darkness crucified the likeness of man
And in so doing lost the battle

God sent His Son in our likeness
So that we would understand His Love

God sent His Son in our likeness
So that we would hear His Voice

God sent His Son in our likeness
So that we would understand
That darkness can be defeated

Thank You Lord, for Your Love
Thank You Lord, for Your Grace
Thank You Lord, for being our Salvation

Please make us worthy of Your Blessings

Amen Amen Amen

God We Need Your Blessings

We are all God's children
We are every where
Every creed and color
God makes no Holy errors

God we need Your blessings
Save us from ourselves
The terror is within us
The hell is where we dwell

We are lost and lonely
Starving and alone
Wandering in this darkness
Looking for a home

We are all God's children
We are every where
Every creed and color
God makes no Holy errors

We victimize each other
No mercy do we show
The darkness, it controls us
Lord, Your love we need to know

We plunder, rape and murder
Everything we see
None of God's creations
Escape our darkest needs

We are all God's children
We are every where
Every creed and color
God makes no Holy errors

Lord in all Your Mercy
Do we make You cry
You love and bless and help us
Yet, we choose our own demise

Cleanse the darkness from our eyes
Breathe Your Spirit in
Pluck us from this madness
Dissolve our unholy sin

We are all God's children
We are every where
Every creed and color
God makes no Holy errors

Remind us You are our Father
The Creator of every child
Teach us Mercy and acceptance
And our demons to exile

God we need Your Blessings
Save us from ourselves
The terror is within us
The hell is where we dwell

Amen Amen Amen

Healed

The demons surrounded me
My heart was griped with fear
My fragile body crumpled
I called the Heavens near

The Holiness of Heaven
Took mercy upon me that day
I was filled with unnatural strength
I faced my demons in that way

I could feel a change within me
I could feel God's Holy Might
I was no longer terrified
By the horror of the night

I looked upon my demons
With eyes that had been healed
To make these wonderful changes
To my Lord I chose to kneel

The demons that had owned me
I now saw through Holy Light
I realized that never again
Would I be a slave to the demons of
the night

For in my misperceptions
For in my fear and pain
I lost control of my life
My Spirit now to regain

Lord lift me from this madness
Carry me through this strife
Bless me with Your Holiness
Breathe within me life

Amen Amen Amen

One Voice Pierced The Darkness

Jesus stood against our foes in darkness
Holiness is His stand
He did what no human army could do
He saved every woman, child and man

One Voice pierced the darkness
One Soul saved the rest
One sent from Heaven
To show us that creation was Blessed

The children cried out with anger
The children cried out with fear
They refused to believe
That Holiness was here

Jesus stood against our foes in
darkness
Holiness is His stand
He did what no human army could do
He saved every woman, child and man

One Light dissolved the darkness
One with Holiness did atone
He saved us from our death sentences
And showed us our Way Home

He taught us with His actions
He showed us as He sees
Darkness can be conquered
If we pray upon our knees

Jesus stood against our foes in
darkness
Holiness is His stand
He did what no human army could do
He saved every woman, child and man

Amen Amen Amen

Help Her Find The Way

I was filled with sorrow when she left
My friend, so lost and alone
I would have traveled all the world
Just to bring her home

I never got to say 'Good bye'
Nor hear what she would say
She left my life so quickly
I wanted her to stay

I heard that she was chasing
Butterflies on that day
The day that she went missing
The day I wanted her to stay

Her memory lingers always
For love, above all, survives
This child sent from the Heavens
God's gifts into our lives

I pray to God to bless her
And all children gone astray
And bring her Home to Heaven
And help her find the Way

Amen Amen Amen

Lord Send Me An Angel

Lord send me an Angel
Send me faith
Send me something Holy to cling to

My light is flickering
The darkness is overwhelming

I am losing the battle
There is so little of me left
I am dying

With the little breath I have
I call Your Holy Name
Please Holy One, forgive me
Please Holy One, save me
Please Holy One, fill me with You

Amen Amen Amen

Coming Home

Seven Little Angels

Seven little Angels, did God send
Seven little Angels sent from above
To promise this world it was not
the end
To sing God's Song of Holy Love

The Angels herald justice, hope and
love
They sang of forgiveness and our
Heavenly Home
They showed us charity, healing and
Holy sight
They said if we reached out to God we
would never want to roam

They said God speaks to us always
But we fail to listen
We push Him away
We choose not to listen

They sang a Song of freedom
Of a Holy Love without end
They said we have a Home in Heaven
And a Father on whom we can depend

They said that God has sent Angels, many
But we do not recognize them when they are here
We fail to see through our darkness
We fail to call the Lord near

We are consumed with the riches of this world
We do not see God's children in need
We distinguish among the vessels
We are driven by hatred and greed

They said to see the Face of God
We have to conquer our fears
To open our hearts and to pray
To call the Lord God near

Amen Amen Amen

Brought Me Back To You

I am dancing on this trail of tears
For death has lost its hold
I sing the Song of Heaven
And follow the melody Home

The tears I cry are Holy
My voice is singing praise
The darkness was defeated
The dead again are raised

My time here was not wasted
I learned my lessons well
I surrendered to my God
And broke the chains of hell

And Glory be to Heaven
And all the Angels who
Helped me on this journey
And God, brought me back to You

Amen Amen Amen

Bring Me Back To Your Arms

God please hear me
I know you have not heard my voice
often
I am filled with guilt and shame
I have made many bad choices in my
life

I have not been a worthy child
And I am not sure You will even listen
to me now
But Lord, I am asking for Your
Forgiveness

Oh God Forgive me
Forgive me
Forgive me

I am so lost
I can not remember the light

I am crippled by the heavy burdens I carry
I am weary

I have sinned greatly
Against my God
Against myself
Against others

I am filled with horror at what I have become
I have allowed myself to be transformed
From the child You created

Please God forgive me
And bring me back to Your arms

Amen Amen Amen

I Choose To Ride With King David

Lord, I choose to ride with King David
To be a warrior of old

To stand against the darkness
To endure the harsh journey that leads Home

To be a tool
To be an instrument
To be a servant
Of my God

To sing
To dance
To ride the victory Home

Amen Amen Amen

Darkness Will Never Stop The Dance

The Spirit consumes me
I dance to the music of Heaven
To the Song of the Lord

I am filled with joy, unspeakable
My life is not my own
The Lord has given me wings and I soar

On His Wings, my spirit sings
My soul takes flight
My life expands the boundaries
Of this world

And I dance
And we dance
And we dance

Heaven sings
God is the Song
God is the Song of creation
God is the Song of Love
God is the Song of all

And I will dance
And we will dance
And we will dance

Let Thy Kingdom come

Amen Amen Amen

God Walk With Me

God walk with me in these dark worlds
Let Your Presence heal
The nature of creation
The covenants are sealed

God walk with me in the worlds of man
By Your Spirit we are atoned
The Heavens cleanse creation
All Glory to Your Throne

God walk with me among the dying
Breathe life back into these worlds
Save Your children, who are crying
The Holy mantle we would gird

God, man can destroy creation
With merely a button of the hand
I call the Heavens to help us
To take a Holy stand

We have been too long without Your Face
Your Presence to many is unknown
Save us from our fates
Save us from the choices we have sown

God walk with us

Amen Amen Amen

The Song Poured Forth
And A Dying World
Was Filled With Holiness
Amen
Amen
Amen

www.ingramcontent.com/pod-product-compliance
Lightning Source LLC
Chambersburg PA
CBHW051711040426
42446CB00008B/821